Wendover

in old picture postcards

by
Colin J. Seabright

European Library – Zaltbommel/Netherlands

Third edition: 1991

GB ISBN 90 288 2920 2 CIP

© 1984 European Library – Zaltbommel/Netherlands

INTRODUCTION

Wendover, variously described as a large village or a small town, at one time sent two Members to Parliament, though these only represented the few hundred people of the Borough, consisting of little more than the four central streets. The out-lying part of the town was administered separately as the Manor of Wendover Forrens with no such privilege. The town stands below the edge of the Buckinghamshire Chilterns where they drop steeply to the Vale of Aylesbury, on the old main road from London to Aylesbury, some 34 miles from the capital and 5 from the county town, at the crossing with the Icknield Way. It is not a simple cross-roads, for the London Road enters one end of the High Street at right angles and Aylesbury Road leaves it similarly at the other, so that all traffic passes through the centre of the town; at one time this brought trade, but now it brings only noise and congestion.

The Icknield Way, the ancient track along the foot of the Chiltern escarpment, leads in one direction past Halton, a village dominated in Victorian times by the influence of the Rothschild family of Halton House and since the First World War by the military establishment. Nearby is Weston Turville, an old village which still boasts many beautiful thatched houses, and was once a major centre for the breeding of Aylesbury Ducks. In the opposite direction, sharing the shelter of Coombe Hill, one of the highest and most popular viewpoints of the Chiltern Hills, Wendover's nearest neighbour is Ellesborough. Here the old cottages and Manor House gather round the church, a prominent landmark from all around. The parish also includes, in a remote hollow of the hills, the mansion of Chequers, now the country home of the Prime Minister. On the ridge behind Coombe Hill is the hamlet of Dunsmore, two inns and a score of cottages around the roadside duck-pond. A descriptive note on the back of one of the postcards states: *The chief attraction of Wendover is undoubtedly the hills which are open to the public, but the rural nature of the town and the many excellent farms in the surrounding neighbourhood are a source of abundant pleasure to visitors,* and throughout the period covered by these pictures the area was a popular 'holiday resort'.

In the sixteenth century, Leland described Wendover as 'a pretty Through-Fayre Towne, having 2 Streets well builded with Tymbre', but some two hundred years later Defoe called it 'a mean, dirty, corporate town'. A county directory, published in Victorian times, includes the following brief history and description of Wendover, *a parish, in the Hundred of Aylesbury, which possesses but few well-built houses and is inconsiderable in point of trade. The manufacture of lace, which was formerly prosperous here, benefits now, comparatively but few persons. Abel Smith, Esq., banker of London, is the lord of the manor and proprietor of much of the land in this parish; his representative holds court for the manor occasionally, and the magistrates for the division* assemble in petty sessions once a fortnight. Wendover sent members to parliament as early as the year 1300; this privilege, which was discontinued for above three hundred years, was restored in the 21st of James I, and the town continued to be represented until disfranchised by the Reform Bill. Hampden, the patriot, represented this borough in five successive parliaments. The parish church of Saint Mary stands about a mile from the town, the living is a vicarage in the patronage of the Crown. There are places of worship for Independents, Baptists and Methodists, and a National school supplied by subscription, and an infants school by Abel Smith, Esq. The market, now but indifferently attended, is held on Monday, and fairs May 13th and October 2nd for cattle.

In 1875 Robert Louis Stevenson visited Wendover on a walking tour, and commented on its setting in the same valley with Great Missenden, but at the foot of it, where the hills trend off on either hand like a coastline, and a great hemisphere of plain lies, like a sea, before one. He was also very impressed by the Red Lion Hotel, but was less enthusiastic about the town, which he described as a straggling, purposeless sort of place, in which everyone seems to have had his own opinion as to how the street should go. It is this lack of regularity and straight-line town planning which gave the old Wendover its character and charm, still very evident today despite the subsequent development on the outskirts.

The pictures in this volume cover the years from the last decade of the nineteenth century to 1930, a period which saw Wendover grow from a quiet country village with a new railway station and a population which had remained steady at around two thousand for several generations, to a busy town with about twice that number of inhabitants, catering also for the needs of the large military base nearby. When Halton Camp was suddenly created in the autumn of 1914 on the slopes of the Rothschild estate overlooking Halton and Wendover, some 25,000 troops were based there, and the peaceful village overnight took on the role of garrison town, with groups of uniformed men to be seen at all times in the previously almost deserted streets. After 1918, Halton became the permanent home of the Royal Flying Corps, then of the Royal Air Force apprentices training school, and although the number of personnel was much less than the wartime peak, the camp remained an important part of Wendover's economy.

In more recent years new residential areas have been developed, particularly along the Aylesbury Road and towards Halton, but very little has been added to the centre of the town, and even less has been taken away, for most of the changes there have been in the form of in-filling, and the great majority of old Wendover, as portrayed on these postcards, remains to be enjoyed today.

WE'RE DOING OUR DUTY

Birds Eye from Monument.

FOR KING AND COUNTRY AT WENDOVER

1. This patriotic card was issued as soon as the military presence was felt in Wendover, using a photograph taken some years earlier, and the copy reproduced here, postmarked January 1916, bears a message from a soldier at Halton to his mother apologising for missing her birthday because 'we are still thick in mud' at the camp. The view from Coombe Hill is said to embrace seven counties, but this picture includes only the local scenery across the golf course in its sheltered valley, and the fields leading to Beacon Hill. Further up the valley, just out of view to the left, is the historic estate of Chequers, recorded in Domesday Book and handed down through many families. The present mansion, built in 1566, was given to the nation by Lord Lee of Fareham in 1920 and has since been used as the official country residence of the Prime Minister.

THE UNVEILING OF COOMBE HILL MONUMENT, NOV. 4TH 1904.

Doulton, Photo

2. The monument on the top of Coombe Hill, often described as the highest point of the Chilterns but actually a few feet lower than the hill behind Halton on the other side of the Wendover Gap, is to the men of Buckinghamshire who fell in the Boer War. The unveiling ceremony in November 1904 was marked by a procession, including a band, which made its way up the hill from Wendover Clock Tower, and was followed by a bonfire on the hill. The main column of the monument was destroyed by lightning in January 1938, but was rebuilt to the original design; more recently the bronze plaque bearing the roll of honour was stolen, and has been replaced by one of stone listing the 148 names of the fallen.

MAKING HISTORY.

[Photo Copyright, J. T. NEWMAN.

Right of Way Dispute on the Wendover Hills.   The Stiles and those who removed them
June 21st, 1906.

3. The summit of Coombe Hill has long been freely, if unofficially, open to the public, but in 1906 Sir John Walton bought a portion of the hill. He erected stiles on some of the traditional paths which the local population considered to be dangerous for women and children, and he put up notices forbidding access across his land to the monument. As he ignored demands for the removal of these obstructions from the long-established rights of way, the men of Wendover banded together to uproot the notices and remove the stiles themselves. After six months of bitter argument Sir John conceded and kissing-gates were erected on his boundaries, some of which, though now very dilapidated, still exist.

4. In the shadow of Coombe Hill, where the Upper Icknield Way crosses the road down the valley from Chequers, is the part of Ellesborough known as Butlers Cross. On the ancient trackway here, with their backs to the hill, stood a group of thatched cottages including this attractive public house, the Rose and Crown. In 'A Random Itinerary', written in 1893, John Davidson relates: *The itinerant left the hill at Ellesborough and rested at the Rose and Crown, a wayside inn with a thatched roof. The sofa in the low-ceiled parlour and the country ale were good. The cheerful ale wife, uncertain of the way, sent in a jolly young countryman, who told him how to go.* The inn and its neighbours, whose doors opened straight on to the roadway, were all demolished after the Second World War and the road widened and straightened.

Butlers Cross. (Bucks.) Coombe Board School.

Photo by Lloyd, Linslade.

5. The hamlet of Coombe, from which the adjacent hill takes its name, is another part of Ellesborough, and consists of a small group of cottages and the village school, standing on the valley road to Chequers. The school, pictured in about 1900, was built by the owners of the Chequers estate in 1839 using the traditional Buckinghamshire building materials of brick and flint, but with a Dutch-style gabled front. With its separate entrances for boys and girls, it provided basic education for the next 130 years for children from all the hamlets that make up the scattered parish of Ellesborough. The building has recently been renovated and extended for use as a residential centre for the Buckinghamshire Girl Guides Association, offering also facilities for camping and other outdoor activities in the adjoining grounds.

Tea at "The Fox", Scrubbs Wood.

6. Dunsmore stands on the breezy ridge which extends back from Coombe Hill, overlooking the main Missenden to Wendover valley, and is in the centre of the most delightful and popular walking country. At one time also known as Scrubwood or Scrubbs wood, the village had, until very recently, two public houses. The Fox Inn is at one end of the village's 'High Street', part of a former green lane along the ridge, where it peters out into a footpath that continues to Coombe Hill and Wendover. The brick and flint Black Horse at the other end, on the path to Hampden is, at the time of writing, being converted into an exclusive restaurant. In this illustration from the turn of the century, the patrons taking tea at The Fox do not appear to be dressed for walking long distances, so have probably arrived by horse-carriage, perhaps on one of the regular tours from Great Missenden station to the Hampden country.

7. Until some thirty years ago there was another inn, the Leather Bottle, about half a mile from Dunsmoor village, which was simply a small cottage in a secluded spot beneath the woods, accessible only by footpaths, where drinks were served in the cottage parlour. Together with some of the cottages in the village which served teas and home-made refreshments, the inns catered for the many hikers who passed through the area every weekend. Courida, a corrugated-iron bungalow with a verandah overlooking Dinah's Hill and the back valley, was one house that provided facilities for visitors. Here patrons could admire the view from deck-chairs on the areas of lawn among cottage-style flower borders featuring magnificent hollyhocks, or play tennis on the private court.

Bird's-eye View of Wendover.

8. This view of Wendover, taken in about 1905, is from the Coombe Hill path, only a short distance above its junction with the Icknield Way at Bacombe Terrace, the roofs of which can be seen over the bushes. Today's view from this point, if one were possible through the trees which have enveloped the lower parts of the hill, would show considerable changes behind the town, where residential development now links up with the military establishment on the slopes of the distant hill. Sheep are still to be seen on Coombe Hill, but they are normally found on the higher open grazing land leading to the summit and the monument, where over a hundred acres has belonged to the National Trust since 1912, when it was given to the nation by Lord Lee, owner of the Chequers estate.

Wendover, Birds' Eye View.

R.J. Morgan, Wendover.

9. In 1917 the slopes of the hills behind Wendover and Halton were covered with wooden huts, replacing the earlier tents, and the trees were being felled to provide props for the dug-outs on the Western Front. A light railway was laid from Halton to the main line at Wendover to facilitate removal of the timber. In this view from the field below the Ellesborough road, due to the 'telephoto' perspective, Halton House and military camp appear to be very close behind Wendover station, where a goods train waits in the siding. The initial opening of the railway was celebrated by a procession from the clock tower, followed by dinner for the old people and tea for the children served in a large marquee in the field by the station.

The Station Bridge, Wendover

10. Wendover station was opened in September 1892 by the Metropolitan Railway, which provided a service from Aylesbury through to the City of London, and which was to lead to the development of commuter traffic and the increased demand for new houses. From the turn of the century the Great Central Railway operated a service over the same tracks, extending to the Midlands and North of England. The illustration shows a London-bound train pulling out of the station which is just beyond the bridge. Metropolitan trains were steam hauled through Wendover until the service was discontinued in 1961, although from 1925 onwards electric traction was used between Rickmansworth and London. The Great Central service, which lost its grand name by amalgamation with other companies and, since nationalisation, has passed under the control of various regions of British Rail, has been cut back to a suburban line, and even that is at present threatened.

11. The Shoulder of Mutton Inn, at the top of Pound Street, was in existence in 1620, when it was shown on a map of the town. Its position near the station gave it the alternative title of Railway Hotel by which it was known for many years and was prominently displayed in this 1918 view. The bridge over the railway line, with its bill-posted wall, leads to the Ellesborough road and the beginning of the track to the summit of Coombe Hill, now part of the Ridgeway long distance path. The ancient pound, from which Pound Street acquired its name, was located just the other side of the bridge off the Ellesborough road, near the present Bacombe Terrace.

at the top of HIGH STREET
WENDOVER, BUCKS.

12. Standing opposite the Shoulder of Mutton, these cottages are the start of the line of attractive buildings, many timbered and with thatched roofs, which fills the south side of Pound Street. This painting, from the end of the last century, displays a degree of artist's licence, for the shadow suggests the sun is shining from the north, but it shows the position of the cottages, on a grassy bank above the road. Pound Street, together with part of the High Street, Back Street and the Tring Road, all follow the line of the Upper Icknield Way.

13. The 'old thatched cottages' of Pound Street date from the early seventeenth century, and have been altered only in detail since this picture of about 1905. The eaves line has been altered in a few places to allow for larger windows to the upper story, and an extension at the extreme right hand end now almost links up with the cottages in the previous picture. Two more gables have been added to the house behind the horse and cart, but, more seriously, the lower end of this block was demolished some years ago to ease the flow of traffic at the corner of South Street. Street lighting was evident by the turn of the century, gas works having been established in Wendover in 1868, later to become part of the Aylesbury Gas Company.

Boddington Hill, Wendover.

14. At the edge of the town along the London Road, which is the continuation of South Street, stands the old Baptist Chapel. The land for the original building, one of Buckinghamshire's first baptist meeting-houses, was granted to the church by the Lord of the manor in 1649. The present building, which bears the legend 'Established 1863' and was extended in 1894, is now well hidden by the adjacent chestnut trees which have grown considerably in the seventy-five years since this postcard was printed. The view is from the railway bridge in Bacombe Lane, looking across the London Road and beyond the chapel to Boddington Hill, on which the crown of trees now spreads further down the slope. In the middle distance the belt of trees marks the line of the Wellhead stream, behind which the new houses of Hale Road can now be seen. The field surrounding the chapel has for many years been a recreation ground, with swings and roundabouts for the local children.

THE OLD LONDON ROAD, WENDOVER.

15. Nearer to the town, this attractive terrace of cottages, pictured in about 1912, still graces the main approach to Wendover from the south. Built at various times in the seventeenth and eighteenth centuries, some with timber framing, they have been smartly re-painted and restored in recent years, and the uneven frontage has been levelled as a narrow pavement separating them from the unending stream of heavy traffic. The oldest cottages, projecting in front of the main line of building opposite the Inn, bore the plaques of the Royal Insurance Company until demolished in recent years, to be replaced by a modern brick house, built in traditional style. The line of hedge on the right hand of the road as far as the King and Queen public house is now the entrance to a residential road on Wichell field, with a modern petrol station beyond.

London Road Wendover.

16. By 1930 the King and Queen was selling the products of the Chesham instead of the Wendover Brewery, and had opened a petrol filling station next door. Here, in front of the old outbuildings of the inn, Regent petrol was dispensed from three hand-operated pumps. Modern garage premises have now replaced all this, but the inn itself, which dates from the early seventeenth century, and the rest of the houses on that side of the street, remain today. Several of the buildings have been used as small shops and businesses for well over a hundred years, including one, near the corner of the High Street, which was the third home of Wendover's much-travelled Post Office. Nearby were the premises of the local ropemakers, whose rope-walk, down by the stream, became the site for the schools.

17. Looking up Pound Street in about 1900, this view shows the areas of grass in front of the houses which are still a feature of many parts of the town, although most of the trees here have now disappeared. In their place the most prominent item of today's view is a giant electricity pylon which towers incongruously behind the houses at the top of the street. South Street leads out of the view, left, sign-posted to Amersham and London; on the far corner of which the gable ended house and its neighbour have now been demolished. A few yards further into South Street a small single-story building, now looking rather neglected, still bears the notice 'Wendover Hall 1860'.

POUND STREET. WENDOVER

18. By the twenties the house on the South Street corner had become Thorne's confectioners shop, with tea rooms. On the other side of Pound Street, on the corner of Dobbins Lane, the shop premises at that time owned by Seago's, still retains the same attractive frontage today. Seago's, with a fine window display of china-ware and a set of chocolate machines outside, had a delivery bicycle, leaning against the side window, and a smart Austin Seven van, parked in front. The shop next-door is still a bakery, but its frontage has been completely rebuilt. At the extreme right hand edge, partly out of the picture, is a once familiar sight, a 'Stop me and buy one' ice-cream delivery tricycle.

Dobbin's Lane, Wendover.

19. This 1900 view is of the beginning of Dobbins Lane, looking out into the top of the High Street, with the out-buildings of the Pound Street corner shop on the right hand side. Some residential development had started at the far end of the lane by this time, and the Mission Church of St. Agnes was built there in 1909. Dobbins Lane has, at times, had two other names, Dame Agnes Lane and Albert Street; the latter was proposed by the local council in honour of the Reverend Albert Smith, Lord of the Manor and Vicar for forty-seven years before the First World War, but rejected by the residents. Between the wars further building took place along the middle of the lane and on side turnings toward the Aylesbury Road, and in consequence the road width has been greatly increased, but the rural atmosphere of the lane has been maintained by the retention of trees, and the presence of sports fields alongside.

WENDOVER. HIGH STREET

20. This large flock of magnificently horned sheep has attracted a few interested onlookers for the 1910 photographer. They are gathered right across the High Street and the Manor Waste, the traditional resting-place for sheep on their way 'on the hoof' to or from Aylesbury Market. The Waste, which adjoins the north side of the High Street, was, from even earlier days, the site of the annual fairs, granted by charter in the fourteenth century. Even up to the early 1900's the May fair saw the area full of animals being bought and sold. The charter also gave Wendover the right to hold a weekly market, and although this had virtually died out well over a hundred years ago, it has recently been successfully revived.

THE POST OFFICE, WENDOVER.

FREEMAN, PHOTO.

21. Wendover's Post Office was originally housed in Brackley's shop at the lower end of the High Street, but was located here, in Freeman's store for many years until 1915. After that it was in premises in South Street before returning to the High Street at Bosworth House, where it remained from 1923 to 1983. In this picture, from the turn of the century, the postal delivery boy is wheeling his official bicycle back to the office, while the drivers and horses of two traps wait patiently outside for their passengers to complete their business.

22. Another view of the Post Office at the beginning of the century, this shows in detail the frontage of Freeman's, the local departmental store. In addition to the Post Office, Freeman and Sons were also, as their sign proudly proclaims, tailors, drapers, chemists, druggists, booksellers, stationers, and agents for Fullers Perth Dye Works! In addition to this, under the name Chiltern Hills Studio, Herbert E. Freeman published many of the earlier cards used in this book. The four splendid gas lamps outside the shop windows were removed around the time of the First World War, but the gable end over the chemists department, which was built to balance that at the other end of the building, still retains its unfinished appearance.

23. Wendover's memorial to those who died in the 1914-1918 War was erected on the open space of the Manor Waste outside Freeman's. In later years it was enclosed in an area of garden, but this was swept away and the whole area renovated and repaved to celebrate the Queen's Silver Jubilee in 1977. In the second half of the nineteenth century, the old lock-up or cage was located in this area which was known for many years afterwards as Cage Bank. This was the site of many civic occasions, such as the return of the local Buckinghamshire Yeomen from the Boer War, when, after arriving in state on the fire engine, they and the welcoming crowds were addressed here by the vicar.

BACK STREET & OLD VILLAGE PUMP, WENDOVER.

24. Looking from the Manor Waste into Back Street, this 1905 card gives a closer look at the old cottages which once adjoined Freeman's shop. The block consisted of three dwellings, of which the lower two are shown, and all three have been demolished, giving access to the modern Holland Close. The outer cottages dated from the early seventeenth century and had visible timber framing, but the middle one had been inserted into the gap some hundred years later. Back Street, for some centuries merely a minor road running parallel to the busy High Street, was originally the main route before the town was created, forming part of the Icknield Way which continued straight ahead into the modern Tring Road.

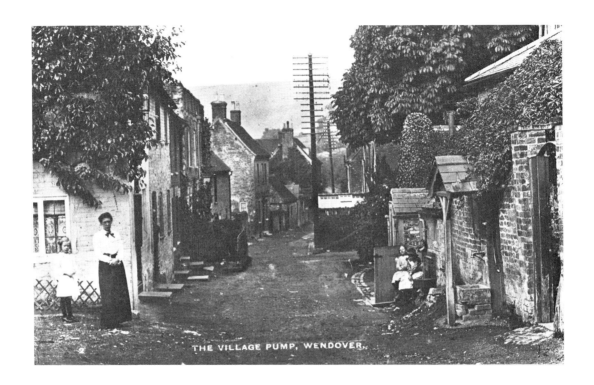

THE VILLAGE PUMP, WENDOVER.

25. This detailed photograph, taken just before the Great War, shows the conditions further down Back Street. The old village pump, with its stone trough and its protective tiled roof, stood immediately outside the back-yard gate of the Two Brewers Inn. Together with another pump in Chandos Place, nearer the bottom of the street, it originally provided water for all the residents of the surrounding dwellings. The pump has now gone, and the outbuildings lining that side of the street have been replaced by modern constructions, as have the single-story buildings well down on the left, but most of the houses remain, one of them still retaining a 'County' Insurance plate.

WAR MEMORIAL & POUND STREET, WENDOVER.

26. The timbered building on the left of this 1922 view up the High Street is Bosworth House, originally built in the late sixteenth century with an over-sailing upper story which has long been underbuilt. When part of the house was converted to create the **Main** Post Office in 1923, a series of fine wall paintings was discovered here. For the next sixty years mail vans using the stabled courtyard of the historic house entered and left through the arch under the gabled room, until the office was closed and replaced by a sub Post Office again, once more at the bottom end of the High Street. The garage at the right hand edge of the picture replaced an earlier forge, and has itself now been replaced by a modern shopping development.

High Street, Wendover.

27. This 1900 view shows King's, another tailors and drapers, who faced their rivals, Freeman's, across the street. The original three-gabled house, forming half of the shop and part of the Inn next door, was built in about 1580 and altered and extended in the late seventeenth century. The King's Head, which was the last public house in Wendover to brew its own beer, has since been demolished and the site is now occupied by a parade of shops. The small children sitting on the kerb outside the shop have their feet in a deep gully which ran almost the whole length of the High Street, with bridges at intervals giving access to the premises.

Wendover Village

28. This postcard, published by the Y.M.C.A. in 1915 for sale to the troops, shows the view down the High Street from the Manor Waste. On the far side of the mud-covered road shop-fitters are working on the house behind the tree, creating an extension of the adjoining drapers shop, which by then belonged to Nicholas Lee, who extended the rivalry with Freeman's by publishing many more local view cards. The appearance of the Manor Waste was to be altered in the late twenties, when business premises replaced the walled garden at the bottom of the slope. An attractive brick building with ornamental chimneys was erected for the National Provincial Bank, whose successors still occupy it today.

Wendover. High Street.

29. Wendover was liberally endowed with public houses, having a total of eleven listed in Victorian and Edwardian times. Two of these stood next door to one another in this block fronting on to the High Street and with their back doors opening into Back Street. The Two Brewers, with prominent bay windows, and the adjoining houses with flights of steps up to their front doors have stood here since the early seventeenth century. With little space at the rear of the premises the first house had a sizeable garden at the side, behind the high brick and flint wall, on which the new bank was later erected. Beyond these, down the street, their slightly younger neighbour, the White Swan, was temporarily without its sign when this picture was taken.

High Street. Wendover.

30. This card of about 1905 shows the view back up the High Street past the White Swan and the Two Brewers, both complete with hanging signs which, unlike today's colourful paintings, only carried the respective names. On the other side of the road the shop at the edge of the picture still stands as Hogarth House, but the site of the orchard beyond it was developed some years ago and is now occupied by the Public Library and car park. Past the orchard the wall of the now-demolished Kings Head Inn then bore a large sign advertising the Wendover Maltings and Brewery which operated from premises at the rear of the inn.

31. Further down the High Street, still sandwiched between it and Back Street, are these old houses, which, over the years, have been converted for use as small shops. The tall building, with second floor dormer windows, housed the watchmaking and jewellery business of E.J. Sharp, who advertised his trade with a giant Ingersoll pocket watch hanging outside. In the early years of the century, when this photograph was published, he also ran a cycle depot in the premises next door. After the Great War he developed quite a busy side-line converting bullet cases, military badges and other wartime souvenirs into brooches.

Red Lion Hotel, Wendover.

32. The Red Lion, one of Wendover's oldest public houses, was built in about 1620, and can claim Oliver Cromwell, Robert Louis Stevenson and Rupert Brooke among its past customers. Stevenson wrote in glowing terms about the comforts of the parlour where he spent an evening on his 1875 walking tour, and was fascinated by the landlord's small daughter. Cement rendering covered the original timbering and brick when pictured here in around 1895, but about a dozen years later this was removed and the timbers renewed and refilled with old bricks. The Red Lion has long been a centre of the social life of Wendover, catering, among other things, for the Masonic Lodge, the Horticultural Association and the Arcadian Bowls Club which used the inn's green up to the end of the Great War.

33. In Victorian days the London coach, 'The Times', operated from the Red Lion to the Old Bell in Holborn. The coach left the yard at seven every morning except Sunday and horses were changed twice en route, at Amersham and Uxbridge; returning to Wendover by nine in the evening. This and the other coach services were superceded by the railway, which offered faster, more frequent and more comfortable travel, but the Old Berkeley Coach operated occasionally until the Great War, although primarily as a tourist attraction, via Great Missenden to Rickmansworth. The picture shows the new 'Tudor' frontage of the Red Lion which was extended over the carriage arch to the hotel's annexe beyond.

34. This 1927 picture of the Red Lion and the bottom of the High Street includes a more modern form of transport, an early motor bus. Red Rose Coaches started operating local bus services from their Aylesbury Road garage in the early twenties and by 1930 Wendover was served by five routes, giving several buses a day to Aylesbury, Chesham, High Wycombe, London and Oxford. The bus is standing outside one of the oldest houses in Wendover, built over four hundred and fifty years ago, but subsequently altered and enlarged, then converted into two small shops. The Royal Commission on Historic Monuments recorded that, in 1912, one of the shops still had the original fireplace and chimney corner seats, then enclosed in a cupboard.

Clock Tower and Literary Institute, Wendover.

35. The Literary Institute, pictured here in the nineties, had been built in 1863 on the site of the old Towne House or market hall which had had a meeting room upstairs over an open piazza and a clock on a bracket over the High Street. This had been demolished some twenty years previously and the space had since been used as a drill ground for the local militiamen. The Institute was built as a memorial to Mr. Abel Smith, Lord of the Manor, by his son Captain Philip Smith, and provided facilities for several generations of Wendover's citizens with a library, reading room and billiard room. After serving for some years as the voluntary-staffed county library, the building is now a dental surgery. Facing the Institute, at the base of the clock tower, was a horse trough, now removed, and the ornamental wall along to the school gates provided seats and a drinking fountain.

THE CLOCK TOWER, WENDOVER.

36. The main part of this building was provided by the Lord of the Manor in 1842 as a small market house to replace the old Towne House across the street. The clock was added later at a cost of ninety pounds, raised by public subscription commemorated by a stone plaque, which reads: 'The Clock is Ye Property of Ye Parish by Contributions from the Vicar, Church Wardens and Occupiers, A.D. 1843.' The ground floor also housed the old stocks and lock-up, which were later moved to the Manor Waste, and it was then the home of the Borough's hand-pumped horse-drawn fire engine. Now disused, there are plans to fit the building out as a Tourist Information Centre. This view was taken toward the end of the Great War, and includes part of a refreshment stall erected on the pavement in front of the drinking fountain.

CLOCK TOWER & OLD WATER MILL, WENDOVER.

37. This view from Aylesbury Street includes Brook House to the left of the Clock Tower, and the old watermill to the right. At the edge of the picture are the Victorian buildings of the National Schools for Juniors and Infants, erected in 1869 and 1879 respectively. The school was one place where the traditional administrative division of the town lingered on, for well into the twentieth century the Headmaster would allow pupils from the 'Forrens' to go home fifteen minutes before those from the 'Borough'. After the Second World War both schools were replaced by new premises elsewhere in the town, and the redundant buildings have been carefully converted into a group of select residences.

38. Very soon after the invasion of Wendover and Halton by the men of Kitchener's Army, the infants school playground was given up as a site for the construction of a Y.M.C.A. Hut. This was opened by Princess Victoria in 1915, to cater for the material and spiritual needs of the new soldiers, with endless cups of tea, and regular magic lantern shows. Beside the school grounds is the entrance to Heron Path or Church Walk, which continues alongside the Wellhead stream for half a mile to the Parish Church. On the other side of the path the butcher's shop with its ventilated wooden shutters is part of a very old cottage. This, and its neighbouring coffee shop have since been converted into a single shop. The iron railings beside the Literary Institute in the corner of the picture remained until the Second World War; on their removal the pavement was re-sited nearer to the building and the road widened.

WENDOVER, BUCKS, CHURCH PATH SHOWING SCHOOLS.

39. Looking back from a little way along the path to the church, this 1910 card shows the rear of the schools. The land on which they stand, beside the Mill Stream, had been the local rope walk, and that manufacture was then moved to a place further upstream. In 1909 school gardens were developed in the neighbouring Millfield, and every one of the two hundred boys and girls then attending the Junior School was encouraged to cultivate his or her own plot. Even though the school population grew considerably, the practice continued until the Second World War, when any produce from the gardens would have helped to augment rations.

40. This little group posed for their photograph in the field beside the stream at the end of the last century. The extent of the school buildings, behind the trunks of the trees, can be appreciated from this direction. Behind the gap is the old watermill, powered by an undershot wheel, which still ground corn until the twenties, and was converted into a house in 1931. This part of the stream, where it widened into the millpond, was the regular home of families of swans. The field now contains a large pre-fabricated building, used by local scouts as an activity centre.

6.4.08

WITCHELL, WENDOVER.

41. The field known now as Witchell, and in the past as Wychewelle Croft, Which Well, and Witch Hill, stretched from the stream to South Street, behind the gardens of the inns and houses of the High Street. The distant scene is little altered today and most of the field is now used as a recreation ground, but the foreground is a residential road bearing the name of the field. Tradition holds that this was the intended site for the parish church, as recorded in a Victorian guide: *It was to have been placed on a field adjoining the town, and there the building of it was begun; but the materials were all carried away in the night by witches, or, as some relate the tradition, by fairies, and deposited where the church now stands. The field where it was to have been built is still called Witchall Meadow.*

The Herring Path,
Wendover
63850

42. The continuation of the path is shown here, at the edge of Witchell, in about 1905, by which date it was illuminated by gas lamps at intervals throughout its length. It is believed to have gained the name Heron Path from the presence of a heronry beside its further stretch, beyond Sluice Cottage towards the church, where the birds were said to stroll along the path. The name was frequently corrupted, as on this card, to Herring Path. The flint building, the other side of which is visible in the view of Witchell, and long since demolished, was a stable serving the animals in the field beyond the iron railings, which, though battered, still remain today.

BUCKS BRIDGE FARM, WENDOVER.

43. A little further along, the path passes, on the other side of the stream, Bucksbridge House and then Bucksbridge Farm, pictured here around the end of the Great War. At the turn of the century netting on the iron fence in the stream had served to contain a flock of ducks to their own stretch of water. Bucksbridge Farm was replaced a few years ago by Heronpath House, and the building operations at that time revealed the remains of a former mill. This was probably the Upper Mill, first recorded in 1542, which had been transferred in early Victorian times to Shift Mill, much further downstream off the Aylesbury Road.

THE SLUICE WENDOVER

44. The water from the springs at Wellhead, after flowing past the town, was used from 1796 onwards to supply the Wendover arm of what was to become the Grand Union Canal. The flow was controlled, not far from the source, by this reservoir and the sluice gates at Sluice Cottage, which was surrounded by well-fenced paths leading, right, to the town, and, left, to the church. Some of these paths have since been closed and the portion in the immediate foreground of this 1910 picture is now hidden between bushes below the houses of Hale Road. The artificial lake, the main feature of this attractive view across the valley to Bacombe Hill, had mostly disappeared by the twenties, and the site is now filled in and covered with an abundance of trees.

ST. MARY'S CHURCH, WENDOVER (IN WINTER)

45. Whether or not the church was moved by the witches or the fairies, or even by the 'Forreners', the eventual site of the building is well outside the Borough in the area of Wendover Forrens. It is in a peaceful rural setting, near the stream and the sheltered Hampden Pond, away from the bustle and traffic of the town. Apart from its architectural features, monuments and brasses, it has another rather unusual claim to fame; in 1799 the Reverend Joseph Smith started, in the vestry, the first Penny Savings Bank in England. This 1900 view is from the end of the Heron path, which here runs between the stream and the pond. The gates were removed from the Lychgate arch some years ago, but otherwise the scene is little changed today.

THE MANOR HOUSE, WENDOVER.

46. The manor of Wendover, at one time held by members of the Hampden family, was bought in 1828 by Robert Smith, a leading banker who was later created Lord Carrington, and has been in the ownership of the Smith family ever since. The manor house, pictured here in about 1900, when it was little more than fifty years old, was built of brick in the Elizabethan style. It stands near the church, on the site of the former parsonage. The building is now used as a school, and has been altered and surrounded by additional modern blocks which hide it from view.

Wendover, Bucks.

47. This 1910 postcard shows the manor house and its then considerable range of outbuildings, as seen from the Hale Road. Some of the smaller buildings have been demolished to make way for the new school additions, and the view from this direction is no longer possible as the viewpoint is now developed with houses and bungalows. At the beginning of the century the manor house grounds were the site of the annual Wendover Flower Show, one of which was due to be staged on the day the Great War was declared, but it was virtually abandoned, not due to the enemy, but because torrential rain flooded the showground.

48. Originally built about three hundred and fifty years ago as four cottages, the building on the corner of Tring Road and Aylesbury Street was used as a shop and bakehouse in the early years of this century. For many years the shop belonged to Morgans, the publishers of this 1915 postcard and most of the other photographic cards of Wendover during the war. The shop appears to be very popular with the soldiers, one of whom is studying the display of comic postcards in the side window. Later refronted with confectionery and tobacco displayed in two bay windows, the frontage has now been restored to the original style as a wine merchants. The right-hand end of the building has since been completely rebuilt, and the remainder renovated with a cement rendering and additional attic windows.

49. This 1927 photograph shows the front of the George Inn which stands at the beginning of Aylesbury Street. Since the War it had lost the enormous gas lamp which used to hang on a bracket over the porch, and the area in front, previously only rough ground with a narrow concrete path to the door, had been paved over and provided with a seat outside. At this date the frontage carried a fine collection of cigarette machines, one advertising free gifts, and another three cigarettes for a penny. Also on the outside wall was a timetable for the Amersham and District Bus Company, who had recently started operating a service from Aylesbury to Amersham which stopped outside.

CORNER HOUSE AND AYLESBURY STREET, WENDOVER

50. At the junction of Back Street and Aylesbury Street stood the Corner House Hotel, built originally as the Junction Inn, an overnight stop for the stage coach from London to Banbury, which entered the yard through a carriage arch where the centre window is now. From 1838 the building was used as a school, with accommodation for the school master, who continued to reside there well into this century even though the classes transferred to the new school as soon as it was built. The hotel, whose facilities included a billiard room, a card room and the Labourers' Club room, where dances were frequently held, continued in operation until well after the Second World War and is pictured here in about 1930. Behind the hotel were the Corner House Tea Gardens with a separate entrance from Back Street, but this area is now a car park serving the adjacent private residences.

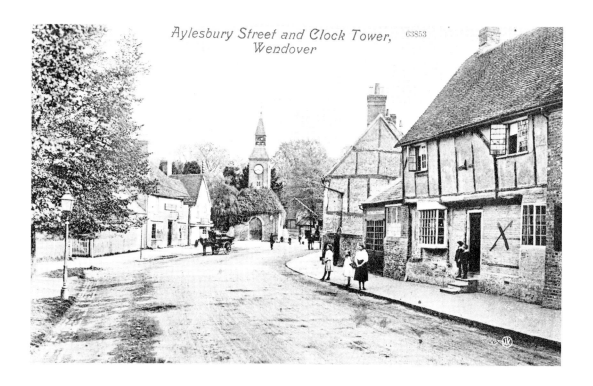

Aylesbury Street and Clock Tower, Wendover

63853

51. Reverting to the beginning of the century, this card shows the first part of Aylesbury Street looking back toward the clock tower and the George Inn. The adjacent garden was replaced by new shop premises built on the site in the twenties. The half-timbered house on the right hand side of the road with its oversailing first floor dates from the sixteenth century; the cross on the card marked the temporary home of the sender who was lodging in Wendover while working in the area. The single-story building next to it was the station for the Wendover Fire Brigade at the end of the last century and well into this, replacing the temporary home of the fire engine under the clock. The fire station was demolished some thirty years ago and a pair of houses built on the site, but the roadside kerb still retains the original access slope to the pavement.

Aylesbury Street, Wendover.

52. The appearance of the sixteenth, seventeenth and eighteenth century buildings which make up Aylesbury Street has changed little in the last hundred years, although some of them have changed their use. The large square carriage arch belongs to the New Inn, an old-established temperance hotel, which is now a private residence known as Sturrick House. Next door to it Chiltern House was, in mid-Victorian times, an 'academy for young gentlemen', run, in his home, by Mr. Bushell, who was later appointed head of the National School. In the late twenties, when this postcard was printed, the road was subject to a ten mile per hour speed limit, announced by round signs, one of which can be seen on the grass verge beside the last tree.

The Old Windmill, Wendover.

53. Just off the Aylesbury road stands Wendover windmill. It was built around 1800, using five hundred tons of bricks brought by donkey from Cholesbury, and boasted the largest cap of any mill in England. A steam engine was introduced in the 1880's to augment the erratic source of natural power and a new engine house with a tall chimney was built after the construction of houses nearby had deflected the prevailing wind. Wind power was then abandoned and this picture was taken just before the final removal of the sails in 1904. The mill continued in operation until 1926 when the prolonged effects of the General Strike prevented the delivery of coal for the engines, and it was converted into a dwelling in 1931. In recent years a new aluminium cap has replaced the traditional black one, and a gallery has been built at the top of the octagonal tower to replace the original one part way up, which had given access to the ends of the sails.

AYLESBURY STREET. WENDOVER.

54. Another wartime picture, this shows the middle of Aylesbury Street with troops and members of the local population taking an evening stroll in a road remarkably free of traffic. Dominating the view, the windmill, now without sails, was a readymade lookout post towering above the surrounding houses, and from here watch was kept for enemy aircraft and Zeppelins. The building to the right, immediately in front of the mill, then stood on an island site within the width of the street at the corner of Wharf Road. This was demolished many years ago, creating a wide area of grass in front of the gardens of The Grange. Wharf Road leads to the now-derelict end of the canal, where much trade and business was once carried out.

Aylesbury Road. Wendover.

55. In the early years of this century this was the limit of Wendover's growth towards Aylesbury, with Victorian houses lining the west side of the road. They were served by their own local shop, the white building with the fancily gabled roof behind the first telegraph pole, and had milk delivered by a little pony-cart carrying a brightly polished churn. The Red Rose garage was established on the opposite side of the road a few years later, and this side is now fully developed with houses on the land down to the old canal. Further building along the road now extends almost to World's End.

Marquis of Granby Inn,

World's End, WENDOVER.

Proprietor: R. J. TURNER.

Marquis of Granby Hotel, World's End, Wendover.

R. J. Turner, Proprietor.

Telegrams:
WENDOVER.
Postal Address.
WESTON TURVILLE.

Large and Small
Parties Catered . .
for.
Tea Gardens, . . .
. . . . Quoits, etc.

Stopping place . . . .
for Parties per . . .
Circular Drives from
Gt. Missenden Station.

Luncheons, Dinners . .
. . and Teas provided.

Pony Trap on Hire.

56. Although the curiously named hamlet of Workd's End, a mile along the Aylesbury Road, never boasted more than a dozen houses, it possessed two public houses, the Marquis of Granby and Wendover's second White Swan, now simply The Swan. This advertising postcard of about 1898 tells everything about the facilities then offered by the sixteenth century Marquis of Granby, and although the building itself remains virtually the same, the setting has changed since then. Traffic now thunders past on a fast stretch of main road where this magnificent array of horse-drawn vehicles stood, presumably on some party excursion.

The Chilterns, Halton, near Aylesbury   Museum and Boys' Gardens

57. One of the houses at World's End is The Chilterns, built in 1867 as the rectory for the parish church of Halton, nearly a mile away. From the end of the century until the early thirties the Reverend Roberts managed a private preparatory school there, and the boys regularly attended his church, where some of them sang in the choir. Their Sunday progress along the lanes must have been a fine, if incongruous sight, as their 'best' uniform consisted of Eton suits and top hats. The house and these out-buildings are now used as a rehabilitation unit for those suffering from spinal disorders, and parts of the grounds are occupied by the greenhouses of the busy garden centre established next door.

WENDOVER, COLD HARBOUR.

58. Probably the most photographed scene in Wendover, the terrace of cottages known as Coldharbour, is here pictured in 1905. Though they lost the prominent shutters from their ground floor windows over the following few years, the cottages otherwise present the same outward appearance today, except for some replacement doors and windows. Past the terrace the rear face of the clock can be seen through the trees in the grounds of Brook House; it is this side of the clock tower which bears the commemorative plaque. A little nearer, hidden among the trees, stands Bank Farm, part of which is believed to be the oldest secular building in the town. The wall and many of the trees have given way to a widened road, re-aligned further away from Coldharbour, leaving space for small gardens and a parking area in front of the terrace.

59. This postcard of Coldharbour from the town end was published in about 1910 as a trade printer's proof, hence the name stamped on it. Coldharbour was shown on the 1620 manorial map, when it is believed to have consisted of five houses, later converted into eleven cottages. They formed part of the dowry given by Henry VIII to one of his brides, giving rise to their alternative name of Anne Boleyn's Cottages. Further properties were added to the terrace, including an Inn at each end, all shown in this detailed view. Clay Lane leads off to the left between the far end of the block and the Congregational Chapel. At one time there was a straw-plaiting school in the lane, and in Victorian times the Rothschild family set up a soup-kitchen there for the poor of the parish.

WENDOVER VIEW FROM "RISING SUN" SHOWING BACOMBE HILL.

60. The Tring Road rises slightly on the way to Halton, and the view back past the Rising Sun Inn looks over the clock tower and the heart of the town to Bacombe Hill, the lower slope of Coombe Hill. The Rising Sun is also known as The Four Seasons, having painted cement panels depicting seasonal scenes on the face of the knapped flint building. The houses opposite the inn were demolished when the road was widened, and as the new estate there is set well back from the road edge, the view is now even more open than it was in 1910. One or two new buildings have been added between the inn and its neighbours, but they do not intrude into the view, being behind the old building line.

61. York Buildings were also known as Thirty Houses, having been built as three terraces of ten; unfortunately there are now only twenty as the furthest block was demolished a few years ago to allow for improvements to the main road. Pictured here in about 1905, the shop at the beginning of the row bore an interesting selection of enamel advertising signs which have long since vanished, but the premises still house a baker's shop. Yet another name for the buildings is Casualty Row, as they originally replaced huts erected by former tenants of Earl Verney who had been evicted from their homes in 1768 for voting against his election nominee. Before the Great War most of the women in the buildings were engaged in straw plaiting, often done in the open doorways, and many of the houses had a straw mill, a small wooden mangle for flattening the strands, fixed inside the front door.

View from Oxon Hill, Wendover,
Showing York Buildings and Bacombe Hill.

26. 9. 68

62. This was the view from the foot of the hills on the way to Halton, looking back over the twists of the old road towards Wendover, shrouded in a smoke haze, and beyond the town to the slopes of Coombe Hill. The Thirty Houses were continued, all along one side of the Tring Road, by two more blocks of cottages and a public house. The latter, in the foreground of this picture, have been bypassed by the improved main road which now leads straight out of the scene by the field, centre right. At the other side of the picture, all the fields have now disappeared under an estate of modern houses which spreads up the lower slopes of the hills.

WENDOVER, BUCKS, LORD KITCHENER'S ARMY ENCAMPMENT,
AT ALTON PARK, M⁹ ALFRED DE ROTHSCHILD'S MANOR.

63. The Rothschild Estate was first used for military purposes in 1912 when land was lent to troops from Aldershot, who, with their three aircraft and an airship, were based there to protect London from enemy attack. Halton Camp was created in the autumn of 1914, when Baron Alfred offered his land at the foot of the Chilterns for military training. In September of that year the sites were measured up and immediately afterwards Territorials arrived from various parts of the country to be billeted at Wendover while they erected the huts and pitched the vast quantity of tents. In the following February Lord Kitchener visited his troops and inspected the camp.

CAMP LIFE AT HALTON PARK.

64. The camp consisted of countless groups, each of about fifty conical tents in orderly rows, interspersed with large marquees and a few scattered wooden huts. Looking from the neighbouring hills the whole scene seemed to consist entirely of canvas, particularly when the smoke from hundreds of stoves obscured the distant view. Throughout its existence the tented camp was. plagued by mud and even before it was fully occupied some of the first arrivals had to be evacuated from their waterlogged tents and billeted in the surrounding area. In December 1915 the sender of this postcard described Wendover as *ankle deep in mud due to the presence of 25,000 troops, many of them from Yorkshire.*

VIEW HALTON PARK NORTH, SHOWING VALE OF AYLESBURY.

65. Gradually the tents were replaced by the wooden buildings shown on this card, but, as the message on the back explains: *This is just a small part of the camp, they won't let them show more because of information to German spies and it would let German aircraft know where the camp is.* However, no attempt was made to camouflage the buildings and the letters Y.M.C.A. were painted on the roof of their hut in the East Camp so clearly that they could be read over a mile away. At the end of the war the camp was used as a demobilisation centre and then, following the death of Baron Rothschild, the estate was sold to the Royal Flying Corps.

66. The Royal Flying Corps and their successors, the Royal Air Force, eventually took over every part of the Halton estate including the mansion itself, which became the Officers' Mess. Aircraft fitters had been trained here as early as 1917, but the first full intake of aircraft apprentices was in 1920, by which time brick-built barracks were replacing the wartime wooden huts. This photograph shows the ceremonial Armistice Day parade in 1924, held on the vast parade ground with a captured German anti-aircraft gun at one corner, overlooked by the new buildings. Among the facilities provided for the residents of the camp was a full size cinema, opened in 1925 and, unlike many of its 'civilian' counterparts, still going strong.

Where Kitchener's Army is Encamped, Halton Manor, Wendover 39886.

67. Halton estate was originally bought by the Rothschild family in 1853 and Halton House was built for them, in the style of a French chateau, in 1884. The grounds were beautifully laid out with lawns, shrubberies and plantations, and in addition to the usual summer-houses and pavilions, included a private skating rink. The gardens were occasionally opened to the public, and were the site of prestigious local events including the week-long Halton Industrial Exhibition during Victoria's reign. Adjoining the mansion was a spectacular domed winter garden, where Alfred de Rothschild staged a variety of entertainments from recitals to circuses, of which he was ring-master. In 1935 the Royal Air Force officers' accommodation was extended by the construction of a west wing on the site of the winter garden.

68. The Wendover arm of the Grand Junction Canal was built primarily as a feeder to carry water from springs in the Wendover area to the summit level of the main canal at Marsworth, a purpose which it never satisfactorily fulfilled as most of the water leaked away into the chalk. However it was made navigable and was used throughout the nineteenth century, principally for the conveyance of straw from Wendover for the draught horses in London, and manure in the reverse direction, and to bring in coal. The canal passed through the middle of Halton where it was crossed by this steep narrow bridge, pictured in about 1916, a dozen years after the navigation was abandoned and partly drained. In 1967 the bridge was demolished and replaced by a modern flat structure.

69. At the beginning of the century a county guide described Halton Church as *charmingly situated, but very ugly within and without.* Modern opinion may not be so scathing, but the construction, of squared stone blocks, does not give a very interesting outward appearance. The church was built in 1813 and was remodelled in 1886 at the expense of the Rothschilds in a style to suit their tastes. Even the setting has now lost some of its attraction; the old cottage in this view from the canal towpath has been replaced, and an estate of modern houses has been constructed almost to the edge of the churchyard.

BIRD'S EYE VIEW. HALTON VILLAGE.

70. The majority of Halton village was built in Victorian times by the Rothschilds, many of the cottages having been completed before the mansion itself. Nearly all the population was employed in the service of the estate, including a full-scale laundry and its private fire service which consisted of eleven men and a horse-drawn fire engine. This 1920 view from the top of the church tower shows the middle of the village, with the canal hidden behind the trees. In recent years much development has taken place in the village, and the houses in this view have been replaced by modern houses and bungalows.

HALTON VILLAGE. 107

71. This view is from Halton church gate looking toward the canal bridge in about 1900. The scene is very different today, as the field to the left of the road and the cottages at the edge have been replaced by modern houses and bungalows. The houses on the other side of the road remain, but with the widening and lowering of the bridge and its approach road, the appearance has been altered considerably. The first house beyond the canal bears a decorative plaster plaque depicting wood-cutters at work, and several other buildings in the village were decorated with similar rural scenes as well as with the Rothschild family arms or motto.

72. Photographed from the hump of the bridge, this view also dates from about 1900 and shows the continuation of the village beyond the canal. The large farmhouse to the left of the road, built in Elizabethan style with twisted brick chimneys, displays its allegiance to the Rothschilds with their arms displayed over the door, on the main wall and on the chimney stack. On the other side of the road the creeper covered building, which was the village school, has been altered only in detail and is now the village hall. The further portion, altered before the Great War by the addition of a large gable, is now a private residence and the building beyond it has been replaced in recent years by the entrance to a new close built on the former playground.

73. Until well into this century, Weston Turville was a fairly scattered village, consisting mainly of thatched cottages at the separate 'Ends', many of them very old. The Royal Commission on Ancient Monuments in 1912 listed nearly thirty from the seventeenth century or earlier, and there were many more of later date. Between the wars expansion started slowly with some infilling, and the orchards and large gardens maintained the very rural atmosphere. More recently development has been much more intense, involving the demolition of some of the older properties. The cottages on the left of this 1905 view of Church End gave way to new houses some years ago, but that on the right has been beautifully restored, revealing its brick and timber construction.

CHURCH END WESTON TURVILLE. 5.

74. Another view of Church End, this was photographed in about 1915 looking in the opposite direction, from the corner of Bates Lane. The Chequers Inn was then hidden behind the thatched block and its neighbours, but following their demolition it is the central feature of the scene today. To the left of the road was one of Weston Turville's many orchards with another behind the facing cottages. A favourite crop in the area was the Aylesbury Prune, which, despite its name, was a cooking plum, of excellent flavour for pies and preserves. After the opening of the railway large quantities of fruit were sent all over the country, and later much jam was made locally for the men at Halton Camp, but the trade virtually ceased after the Second World War.

75. This view should bring back memories to those who were brought up in Weston Turville, for the building in the centre is the former village school. This was demolished a few years ago and the site is now occupied by modern houses, with another new estate on the opposite side of the road. Beyond the school the old school house remains today, as does the thatched building in the foreground. Built in the seventeenth century as one cottage, it was divided into two tenements at the time of the picture, but has now been restored to a single dwelling.

Aylesbury Ducks at home. Weston Turville

76. Toward the end of the nineteenth century Weston Turville replaced Aylesbury itself as the main breeding centre for Aylesbury Ducks. In 1900, when this card was published, business was at its peak with 25,000 birds sent to market from the village in one season, and the industry declined only slowly until the twenties. The ducks' life was not as idyllic as this scene might suggest, as the ducklings were mostly reared in pens, fed a special diet to fatten them quickly, and only allowed one swim before slaughter at the age of eight weeks. The swim was to improve the quality of the feathers which, together with the meat, were in great demand at the London markets. The pictured pond is actually in the roadway of Main Street, and the site is now marked by a bus layby. Almost opposite the end of the cottages now stands the modern parade of village shops.